I0786914

traditional turned trendy

Trends turn on a dime, but that's what I love about these four wreaths. These classic designs never really go out of style because it's so easy to update them with modern materials. They're always on trend!

grapevine wreath

Grapevine wreath forms are a favorite. They're inexpensive, easy to work with, and the vines allow you to quickly attach florals and all sorts of decorative items to transform these beauties for any season!

Supplies

- 24"-diameter grapevine wreath form
- 2 varieties of leaf stems or vines
- 2 varieties of floral sprays
- 2 floral stems with large blooms
- 4 yards of 2"-wide wire-edge ribbon

Tools

- Floral snips
- Floral wire
- Glue gun and hot glue
- Ruler

1. **Trim the leaf stems.** Trim the leaf stems into smaller individual pieces. If using vines, trim them into 8" to 10" long pieces.

2. **Attach the leaf stems.** Place the leaf stems on the wreath form to get an idea of where you'd like to attach them. Then, weave each stem into the wreath form and secure it with floral wire. Cover about three-quarters of the wreath form with leaves.

3. **Attach the florals.** Attach several large flower buds with floral wire, grouping them on one side of the wreath form. Use hot glue for extra security or to position the blooms facing a specific direction. Add the floral sprays and any remaining leaf stems for fullness and to fill in any gaps in the design. Secure them with floral wire.

4. **Finish with a bow.** Tie the ribbon into a bow with multiple loops and attach it with floral wire.

RIBBON FULLNESS

If your ribbon doesn't have wire edges and is falling flat, cut strips of clear vellum or acetate slightly narrower than the width of your ribbon. Form the strips into loops, securing them with double-sided tape. Insert the vellum loops into the loops of your bow to help them stand up. Secure the vellum to the ribbon with additional pieces of double-sided tape as needed.

burlap rag wreath

It doesn't get much easier than a rag wreath. If you can tie a bow, you can make this design!

Supplies

- 20"-diameter wire wreath form
- 2 yards burlap
- Word, letters, or phrase (like "Welcome")
- Coordinating craft paint

Tools

- Self-healing cutting mat
- Rotary cutter
- Clear ruler
- Paintbrush
- Mini paint palette
- Glue gun and hot glue

welcome

LESS MESS FABRICS

Burlap sheds and can make a great mess. If you don't care for the strings and fuzz, choose another fabric in a nice solid color to create a similar effect without the mess.

1. **Cut the burlap.** Using the rotary cutter, cut the burlap into 1" x 9" strips.

2. **Tie on the burlap.** Starting with the inner band, tie a burlap strip onto each band of the wreath form. Repeat, working in columns. As you tie the burlap onto each band, slide the pieces close together to close any gaps and hide most of the wire.

3. **Paint and attach the letters.** Apply two to three light coats of paint to the lettering. These letters are often made of thick cardboard. To keep them from buckling, be sure to avoid drenching them with paint. Take your time and apply multiple coats, allowing each coat to dry completely. Use clear fishing line or hot glue to attach the letters to the wreath.

palm frond wreath

Vine wreath forms are very common, available in every craft store. Give them a modern flair with large palm fronds and fern sprays—perfect for coastal homes and summer party décor!

Supplies

- 18"-diameter vine wreath form
- Palm fronds
- 2 varieties of fern stems

Tools

- Glue gun and hot glue
- Floral snips
- Floral tape that matches the wreath form
- Clear fishing line (optional)

1. **Trim the ferns.** Using the floral snips, trim the ferns into smaller individual pieces as needed for your design.

2. **Shape and attach the greens.** Mold the stems of the greens to the shape of the wreath form. Trim any stems that are too long. Then, arrange the greens in layers and glue the stems to the wreath form, tucking the palm fronds between the ferns.

3. **Wrap the stems.** Wrap the stems of the greens with floral tape that matches the wreath form.

TIP

If your palms or greens are heavy, tie them to the wreath form with clear fishing line between Steps 2 and 3 for extra security.

grapevine sunburst wreath

Sunburst wreath forms are my go-to for designs that I want to be large and full all the way around. These forms provide lots of surface area for greenery, big blooms, and any other decorative items you want to embellish them with!

Supplies

- 24"-diameter grapevine sunburst wreath form
- 1 eucalyptus stem
- 2 to 3 varieties of leaf stems or other greens
- 2 to 3 floral stems with large blooms
- 4 yards of 2"-wide wire-edge ribbon

Tools

- Floral snips
- Floral wire
- Glue gun and hot glue
- Ruler
- Scissors

1. **Trim and attach the leaf stems.** Trim the eucalyptus and leaf stems into individual pieces 6" to 8" long. Place the stems on the wreath form to get an idea of where you'd like to attach them. Then, use hot glue to attach the stems around the entire wreath form.

2. **Attach the florals.** Leaving a 5" space for a bow, add the large flower buds. Use floral wire to attach them to the inner ring of the wreath form. Add hot glue for extra security or to position the blooms facing a specific direction.

3. **Fill in the design.** Add any remaining leaf stems to add fullness and fill any gaps in the design. Secure them with floral wire or hot glue as needed.

4. **Finish with a bow.** Tie the ribbon into a bow with multiple loops and attach it with floral wire. Cut a triangular notch into each end of the ribbon to keep it from unraveling.

not the usual suspects

Wreaths come in all shapes, sizes, and materials. There is no need to limit yourself to round shapes and open centers! Feel free to get creative and be a bit unconventional with your designs!

chicken wire

Farmhouse home décor style has made this rustic material new again. Used in small amounts, it can be the perfect form for sprays, silk florals, and even felt petals.

Supplies

- Chicken wire wreath form
- 2 varieties of leaf stems
- 1 cotton stem
- 1 medium-sized floral stem

Tools

- Glue gun and hot glue
- Clear fishing line
- Floral snips
- Scissors

MAKE YOUR OWN

With vines from either your yard or the craft store, floral wire, floral tape, chicken wire, wire cutters, and a marker, you can make your own wreath form in any size you'd like. Form the vines into a ring, overlapping the ends and securing them with floral wire. If the edges are raw and unseemly, cover them with floral tape in the same color as the vines. Mark and cut the chicken wire to fit the center of the ring. Attach it to the back of the ring with floral wire.

1. **Shape the leaf stems.** Trim the leaf stems into individual pieces. Using the outer edge of the wreath form as a guide, mold the leaf stems to the shape of the wreath. Trim off any excess stems.

2. **Attach the leaf stems.** Glue the leaf stems around the outer edges of the wreath, holding each stem in place for about 15 seconds. For extra security, tie each stem to the wreath with clear fishing line, especially if the wreath will be displayed outdoors.

3. **Attach the cotton and floral stems.** Repeat Step 2 with the cotton and floral stems, tucking them behind the leaves to hide any glue or fishing line.

geometric shapes

You might be surprised to learn that these lovely gold geometric shapes are nothing more than office supplies—just pretty paper and mail trays. I've always loved office and back-to-school supplies, so I often peruse those aisles when I'm shopping. These little gems were too good to pass up, and they make a sweet addition to any workspace or feminine bedroom!

Supplies

- Paper trays in three sizes
- 1 leaf stem
- 2 floral sprays
- 1 floral stem with flower buds

Tools

- Glue gun and hot glue
- Clear fishing line
- Floral snips
- Scissors

1. **Shape the leaf stems.** Trim the leaf stem into individual pieces and mold them around the edges of the trays. Leave some of the pieces long and wispy for flair and color.

2. **Attach the leaf stems.** Glue the leaf stems to the trays, holding each one in place for about 15 seconds. For extra security, tie the stems to the trays with clear fishing line.

3. **Attach the florals.** Repeat Steps 1–2 with the floral sprays, tucking them behind the leaves to hide any glue or fishing line.

4. **Finish with flower buds.** Add large flower buds to the base of the bundles on each wreath. For the largest wreath, place the bud in the center of the design for symmetry.

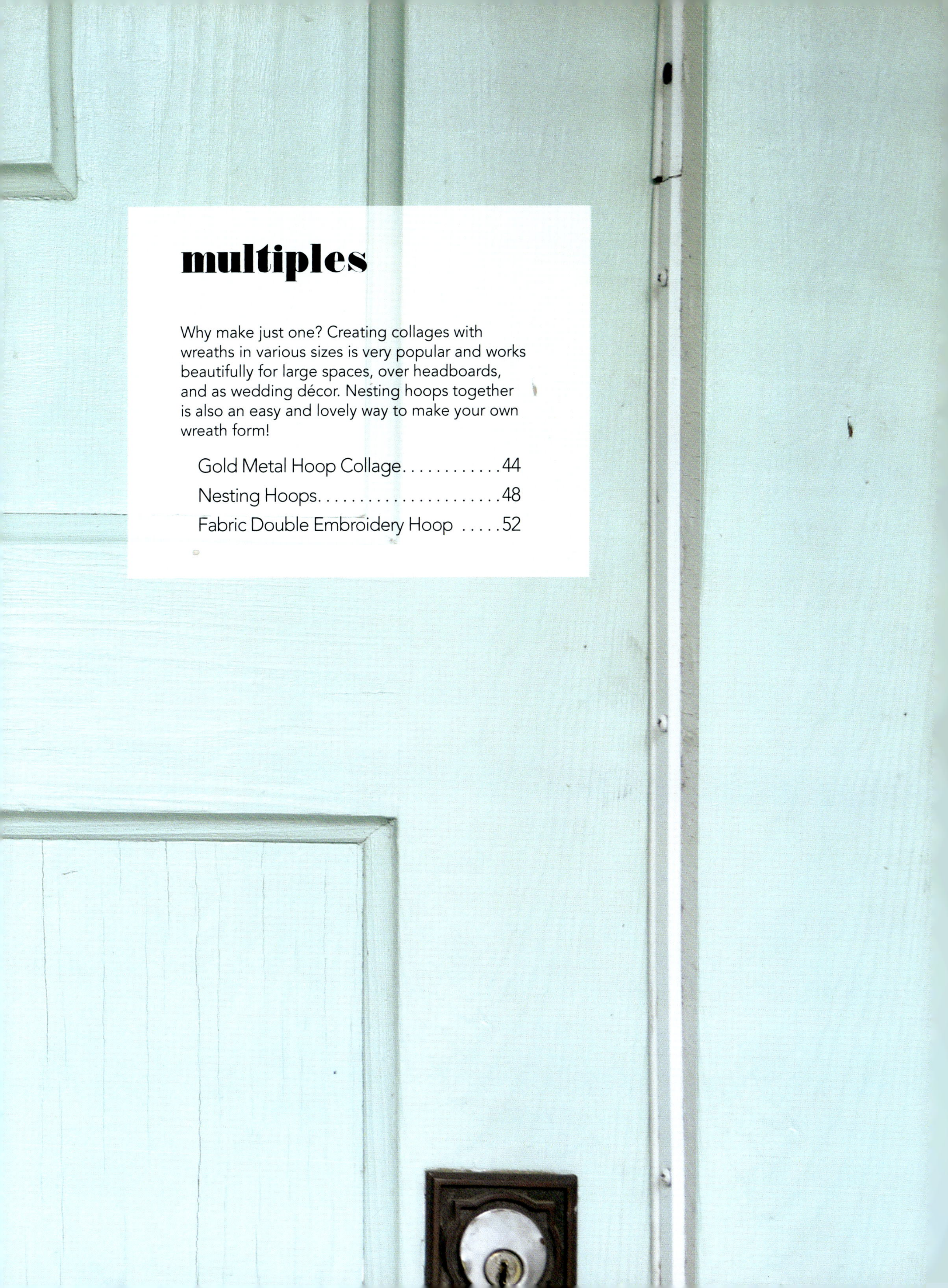

multiples

Why make just one? Creating collages with wreaths in various sizes is very popular and works beautifully for large spaces, over headboards, and as wedding décor. Nesting hoops together is also an easy and lovely way to make your own wreath form!

gold metal hoop collage

These metal hoops are often used for macramé and are easily found in various sizes at your craft store. They also make perfect wreath forms for faux and fresh flowers!

Supplies

- One 12"-diameter gold ring
- Two 6"-diameter gold rings
- 2 varieties of floral sprays
- 1 floral stem

Tools

- Floral snips
- Glue gun and hot glue
- Clear fishing line
- Scissors
- Floral tape (optional)

1. **Shape the florals.** Trim the florals into individual pieces as needed for your design. Using the rings as a guide, mold the stems of the florals to the shape of the rings.

2. **Attach the florals.** Using the hot glue and clear fishing line, secure the florals to the rings. For the large ring, work out from the center to create a symmetrical design. For the smaller rings, work from the center out to the right.

TIP

Tape if needed. Hot glue doesn't always stick to metal. If you find this is the case, wrap the metal hoops with floral tape and hot glue the florals to the tape.

nesting hoops

Stacking or nesting hoops is a darling way to make a large wreath without losing too much space in the center. You can use oval hoops for this design, too. Especially if you'd like to include lettering or a saying in the design.

Supplies

- One 23"-diameter embroidery hoop
- One 12"-diameter embroidery hoop
- Twine
- 2 varieties of floral sprays
- 1 floral stem with large blooms
- Raffia

Tools

- Floral snips
- Glue gun and hot glue
- Clear fishing line
- Scissors

1. **Attach the hoops.** Place the smaller embroidery hoop inside the larger one and secure them together with twine. Hot glue one end of the twine to the edge of one hoop, wrap the twine around both hoops several times, trim the twine, and hot glue the loose end in place.

2. **Separate the florals.** Trim the florals so you have stems with leaves only and stems with both leaves and flowers.

3. **Begin attaching the florals.** Using hot glue, begin attaching florals to each hoop, starting with the sprays and flat leafy stems. Use the florals to cover the connectors of each embroidery hoop.

TIP

Embroidery hoop connectors are the widest area of the hoop, so they're the best place to layer and secure florals. Plus, it's a great way to hide the connectors in the finished design!

4. **Continue building the design.** Continue adding florals to each hoop, building the arrangement from the center outward for a symmetrical design. Use hot glue and clear fishing line or raffia to attach the florals.

5. **Top with large flowers.** Hide the stem ends at the center of each arrangement by gluing a large flower over them.

fabric double embroidery hoop

Creating a fabric background for your wreath is a creative way to introduce unique colors and patterns to your design. Choose a fabric that fits your style and have fun adding matching florals.

Supplies

- ½ yard fabric
- One 12"-diameter embroidery hoop
- One 8"-diameter embroidery hoop
- 1 leaf stem
- 1 large flower bud
- White foam
- Mod Podge

Tools

- Glue gun and hot glue
- Self-healing cutting mat
- Rotary cutter
- Pencil
- Clear ruler
- Wax paper (optional)

1. **Trace the foam backer.** Place the embroidery hoops on the foam with the smaller hoop inside the larger hoop. Use the ruler to make sure the space between the two hoops is even. Trace around the outside of both hoops.

2. **Cut out the foam backer.** Using a rotary cutter, cut out the ring you traced on the foam. Place the embroidery hoops on top. The foam should fit nicely behind them without any excess showing around the edges. Trim If necessary.

3. **Cut the fabric.** Using the foam ring as a template, use the rotary cutter to cut the fabric to the same size.

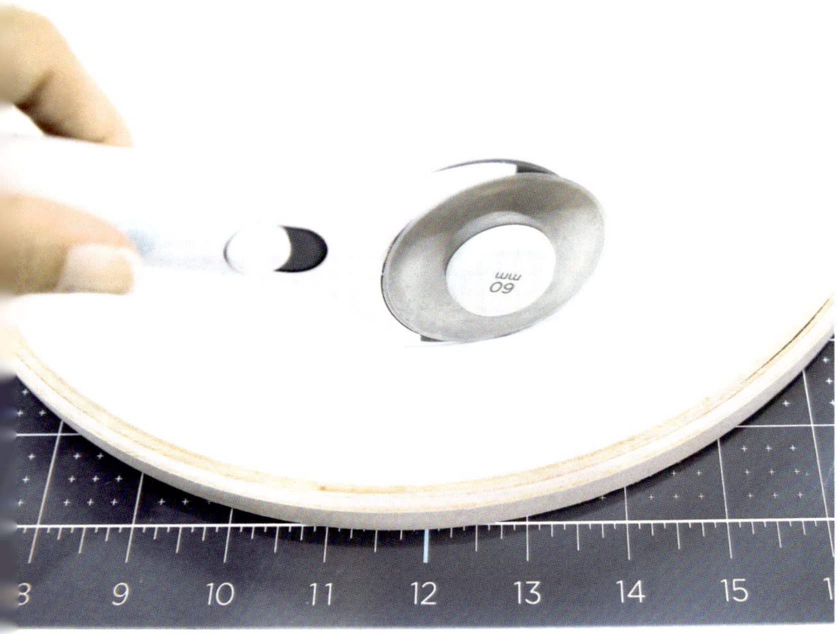

4. **Attach the fabric.** Apply Mod Podge to the foam ring and attach the fabric. Work in small sections, about a quarter of the ring at a time, so the Mod Podge doesn't dry before you attach the fabric. You can use wax paper to protect your work surface.

5. **Attach the embroidery hoops.** Glue the embroidery hoops in place on top of the foam and fabric backer. Position the connector of the large embroidery hoop at the top of the wreath and the connector of the small embroidery hoop to one side.

6. **Attach the florals.** Use hot glue to attach the florals to one side of the wreath, hiding the connector of the small embroidery hoop.

natural wonders

There are no better craft supplies than the ones God made himself. Nature holds so many treasures. Of course, there are countless beautiful and fragrant flowers, but there are also things like corn husks, pine cones, cotton, feathers, and so much more that will last and last.

corn husks

You may have purchased dried corn husks for your favorite tamale recipe, but have you ever considered using them as craft supplies? They're easy to cut, easy to mold, and interesting to behold!

Supplies

- 12"-diameter foam wreath form
- 8 oz. pack of corn husks (about 50 total)
- 1 floral spray
- 1 floral stem with large blooms (optional)

Tools

- Glue gun and hot glue
- Floral pins
- Floral snips
- Scissors

1. **Prepare the corn husks.** Separate the corn husks and remove any corn silk. Group the husks by size.

2. **Attach the corn husks.** Pin a corn husk to the wreath form, angling it outward slightly. Place the pin about 2" from the bottom of the husk. Pin another husk in place, overlapping the first husk to hide the pin. Repeat, using husks of the same size until half of the wreath form is covered.

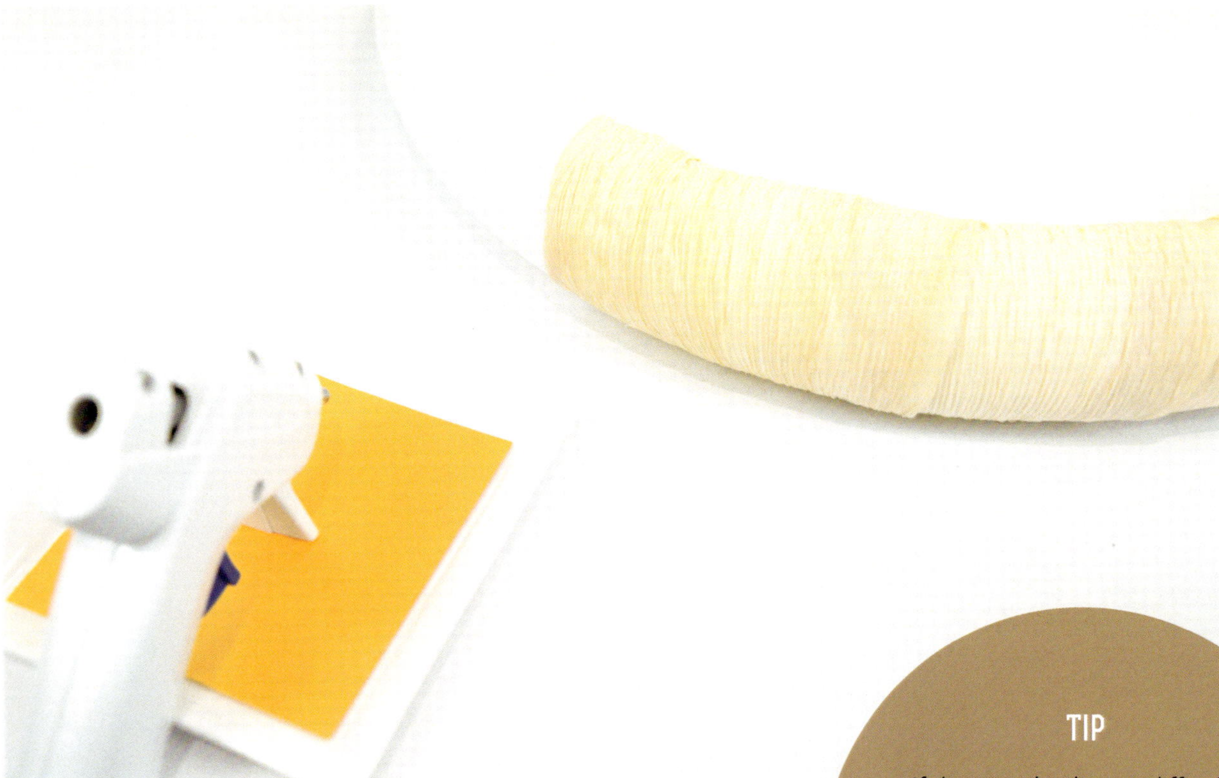

TIP

If the corn husks are difficult to wrap around the wreath form, dampen them slightly and heat them in the microwave for 20 seconds. This will make them more pliable so you can wrap them around the wreath more easily.

3. **Wrap the wreath form.** Cover the rest of the wreath form by wrapping husks around the form and securing them at the back with pins. Each husk should slightly overlap the one before it to cover the form completely. Trim away any excess with scissors.

4. **Trim and attach the palm shapes.** Using scissors, trim several husks so they resemble palm branches. Hot glue them in place over the husks you pinned on in Step 2. Overlap the husks and angle them inward and outward slightly to create fullness and flair.

5. **Attach the florals.** Trim the floral sprays into smaller individual pieces as needed for your design. Hot glue them to the wreath, tucking them into place between the palm-shaped husks. If desired, finish with a few large flowers.

succulents

These plants are not only popular in the west, but they've also become wildly popular all over. Make hanging planters like this one, or infuse faux succulents into any number of fabric, vine, or wire wreath types.

Supplies

- Hanging metal floral tray
- Floral foam circle that fits your floral tray
- Faux succulents or air plants
- Preserved moss

Tools

- Glue gun and hot glue
- Floral pins

1. **Attach the foam.** Use hot glue to secure the foam circle inside the floral tray.

2. **Cover the foam.** Cover the foam with moss, securing it in place with floral pins.

3. **Add succulents.** Starting with a large succulent in the center of the design, insert the stems of the succulents into the foam at various heights.

MAKE A LIVING WREATH

You can use air plants (plants that don't require soil) to make a living wreath. Instead of moss, fill the area around the foam circle with small pebbles. To water, wet the roots every two weeks, but don't submerge in water.

cotton yarn weave

Soft, fluffy cotton yarn gives your wreath a delicate touch that's perfect for bedrooms and nurseries. Weaving, braiding, and looping are all popular ways to work with yarn.

Supplies

- 20"-diameter wire wreath form
- Bulky cotton yarn
- 1 floral spray
- 1 cattail floral spray
- Feathers
- Spray paint matching your yarn

Tools

- Glue gun and hot glue
- Floral snips
- Scissors
- Clear 18" ruler

1. **Paint the wreath form.** Spray the wreath form with the spray paint you've chosen to match your yarn. Allow it to dry completely, preferably overnight.

2. **Trim the yarn.** Cut the yarn into 24"-long strips. It's much easier to weave with smaller lengths of yarn than to work off the skein.

3. **Attach and weave.** Wrap the end of a yarn strip around the outer band of the wreath form and glue it to itself. Don't glue the yarn to the wreath form—you want to be able to move it around the wreath as you work. Weave the yarn over and under the metal bands of the wreath form, sliding the rows close together to close any gaps and hide most of the wire. When you get to the end of the yarn, wrap it around the inner band of the wreath form and glue it to itself, trimming away any excess.

4. **Add the florals and feathers.** Trim the florals into individual pieces and attach them to one side of the wreath. Secure them to the back of the wreath with glue or by tucking the stems under the yarn. Add feathers or a large flower to the front of the wreath at the base of the floral bundle.

TIP

Be careful not to twist the yarn as you weave so it comes out nice and flat in your finished design.

making old things new

Why get rid of things that can be made beautiful again—old bike spokes, wagon wheels, berry barrel lids, and more. Vintage items have so much character and often a story or two to tell. Upcycle them into a beautiful design filled with character.

hello

wagon wheel

A lovely worn wagon wheel makes a perfect home décor item for the ever-popular farmhouse style. If you don't have a wagon wheel available and can't find one at your local craft store or an estate sale, an old bicycle wheel rim with wire spokes is the perfect substitute!

Supplies

- Wagon wheel
- 2 varieties of floral stems
- 2 varieties of floral sprays
- Vine florals
- Large flower buds
- Word, letters, or phrase (like "Hello")
- Coordinating craft paint

Tools

- Glue gun and hot glue
- Wood glue (optional)
- Clear fishing line
- Floral tape (optional)
- Floral snips
- Scissors
- Paintbrush
- Mini paint palette

hello

1. **Attach the florals.** Trim the florals into individual pieces and glue them in place around the wagon wheel. Start with a layer or two of stems and sprays. Then add the floral vines on top, removing any excess stems as needed. Finish the design with the large flower buds, using them to hide the stems of the previous layers. Insert any remaining sprays into the finished design to add fullness.

2. **Paint the letters.** Apply two to three light coats of paint to the lettering. These letters are often made of thick cardboard. To keep them from buckling, be sure to avoid drenching them with paint. Take your time and apply multiple coats, allowing each coat to dry completely.

3. **Attach the letters.** Use clear fishing line or wood glue to attach the letters to the wagon wheel opposite the florals.

TIP

If you happen to damage the tip of one of your floral sprays or stems and it will show in the finished design, wrap it with matching floral tape.

bushel lid

You can't go wrong with wood, especially weathered wood. The darling bushel basket lid I used for this design sat in a North Carolina barn for more than 50 years after the farmer used the basket for grain storage. Now it has found new life as a beautiful home décor piece.

Supplies

- Bushel or barrel lid
- 1 variety of floral spray
- 1 flowering vine
- 1 large floral stem with flower buds
- Word, letters, or phrase (like "Hi")
- Coordinating craft paint

Tools

- Glue gun and hot glue
- Clear fishing line
- Wood glue (optional)
- Floral snips
- Scissors
- Paintbrush
- Mini paint palette
- Paper towel

1. **Attach the sprays.** Trim the floral sprays into individual pieces and glue a layer or two in place around the bushel lid.

2. **Attach the vine and florals.** Add the flowering vine on top of the sprays. Finish the design with large flower buds, using them to hide the stems of the previous layers. Insert any remaining sprays into the finished design to add fullness.

3. **Paint the letters.** Apply a light coat of paint to the letters. Before it has a chance to dry completely, wipe some of the paint away with a paper towel to create a washed, distressed look.

4. **Attach the letters.** Use clear fishing line or wood glue to attach the letters to the bushel lid opposite the florals.

about the author

Kim Wilson Byers is the creative director and owner of The Celebration Shoppe, a graphic design studio and lifestyle blog. Kim shares crafts, entertaining ideas, and recipes with thousands of readers every day.

Kim has been blessed to have her designs, party ideas, and recipes featured in a number of nationally published magazines, including *Parents*, *Better Homes and Gardens*, *All You*, and *Pregnancy*, to name just a few.

In addition to sharing creative and easy craft tutorials with her readers, chatting them up on Facebook, and sharing videos of her day-to-day on Instagram, Kim also designs paper crafts for select craft companies and has her own line of party crafts and cake kits.

Kim lives on 20 acres nestled in the rolling hills at the tip of the Appalachian mountain range in Alabama with her husband of 20 years and her two sons.

Kim holds a master's degree in Marketing and spent the first 10 years of her career in investment management, only to have her perspective on what's important change in an instant when her boys were born. Kim still works more hours than is often reasonable, but from her home studio, where being a mom can take precedence anytime she's needed.

A crafter, entertaining expert, and graphic designer, Kim shows thousands of readers everyday tips and ideas about making both big and small moments personal and memorable. In these pages, she will inspire you to make your day.

Made in U.S.A.

Library of Congress Control Number: 2019945412

Instructional photography by Kim Wilson Byers.

Copyright © 2019 by Leisure Arts, Inc., 104 Champs Blvd., STE 100, Maumelle, AR 72113-6738, *www.leisurearts.com*. All rights reserved. This publication is protected under federal copyright laws. Reproduction or distribution of this publication or any other Leisure Arts publication, including publications which are out of print, is prohibited unless specifically authorized. This includes, but is not limited to, any form of reproduction or distribution on or through the Internet, including posting, scanning, or e-mail transmission.

We have made every effort to ensure that these instructions are accurate and complete. We cannot, however, be responsible for human error, typographical mistakes, or variations in individual work.

Production Team: Technical Editor – Katie Weeber; Graphic Designer – Kate Moul; Photo Stylist– Lori Wenger; Photographer – Jason Masters